THE TRUTH ABOUT FONZIE

by PEGGY HERZ

SCHOLASTIC BOOK SERVICES
New York Toronto London Auckland Sydney

For Debbie, Nancy, Steve, Mark, Jon, Peter, Sharon, and all the other young people who kept **Happy Days** alive while it was still trying to find itself—and who, from the beginning, saw something very special in a modern-day free spirit called The Fonz.

And for Henry Winkler, who really is a modern-day free spirit, and who knows from his mind and heart what being cool is all about.

 Published by Scholastic Book Services, a division of Scholastic Magazines, Inc.

12 11 10 9 8 7 6 5 4 3 2 10 6 7 8 9/7 0 1/8

06

Printed in the U.S.A.

CONTENTS

Henry Winkler as Fonzie in *Happy Days*.

A Cold Winter Day and Lunch with Henry Winkler

New York wasn't at its best the day I met Henry Winkler. It was December 27, 1974 — a dark, dreary winter day. It was probably snowing and beautiful out in the surrounding countryside. But in the big city, it was simply cold and raw. As I walked uptown, I tried not to look at the limp Christmas decorations or the chilled-looking people hurrying along the street.

Henry and I were to meet for lunch at an Italian restaurant on Central Park South. I didn't know Henry then and didn't know much about him. I had read his network biography, but that didn't tell me much. Network biographies give basic facts about a person — but they don't give you any sense of what a person is really like.

I had also watched *Happy Days* several times, but I wasn't really sold on it. The show had done well enough to stay on the air, but I hadn't found it to be very exciting. It was pleasant enough, but it didn't say much to me.

I didn't know then that all of this would change. During the next 18 months, I would learn a great deal about Henry Winkler. I would begin to consider him both a superb performer and a good friend. I would watch *Happy Days* get better and better, and begin to zoom upwards in the ratings. I would begin to plan my own schedule so that I didn't miss a weekly episode.

Henry and I have met several times since that first luncheon. We have talked at length about a number of subjects — or we have just sat quietly and listened to the music he loves so much. All our recent meetings have taken place in Los Angeles, where Henry now lives and works. But I'm glad I met him in New York, for Henry grew up in New York — and he is very much a product of his hometown.

New York isn't like any other city in the world. It has all the problems of big cities anywhere — crime, dirt, congestion, and all the rest. Its people often seem cold and unfriendly. They rush around and bump into each other with their elbows and their umbrellas, but not with their hearts or their minds.

At the core of the city, however, there is a solid bedrock of great creative talent in many varied fields — from finance and fashion to publishing and performing. New York isn't a city of "overnight" successes. You want to make it in New York? Then you dream your dreams, but you also work and study and then work some more. That's exactly what Henry Winkler did.

The Fonz has become the coolest, most popular character on television today. It didn't happen by accident. It happened because Henry Winkler knew what he was doing. He is very serious about his work. He studied for years to be an actor. He is totally dedicated — to his profession and to himself.

Henry is tough, but he is also very gentle. He is cool about his fame — and passionate about his work. Some Hollywood performers brag that they have never taken acting lessons. That isn't Henry's style. He studied, all right, and now he's turned a high school dropout named Arthur Fonzarelli into the biggest thing to hit TV since the invention of the picture tube.

How did it all happen? Why have Fonzie and *Happy Days* skyrocketed to such heights of popularity? It's quite a story — and many people had a hand in it all. Probably the most amazing aspect of the whole story is that Henry got the part of Fonzie in the first place. He wasn't what the producers had in mind at all. He got the part at the very last minute. At first, it wasn't meant to be a big part, but Henry changed all that.

To see how, let's turn the clock back a few years.

Finding Fonzie Wasn't Easy

One day several years ago, on an airplane going from New York to Los Angeles, producer Thomas L. Miller got to talking with Michael D. Eisner, vice-president of program planning and development at ABC. During the flight, the two men came up with an idea for a new TV show — a comedy about a family living during the 1930's. The more they talked, the more excited they became.

"I can't remember which of us came up with the idea first," Miller admitted, "but we both liked it. Eisner asked me who I would want to create such a show. I told him Garry Marshall was the best comedy writer around."

By the time the plane landed, Miller and Eisner were convinced they had a hit on their hands. The public, they agreed, was ready for a comedy about people living during a time when life seemed simpler and the pace was slower.

Miller went to Garry Marshall with his idea. Would Marshall write a script about a family living in the 1930's? Marshall said no.

"They wanted me to do a *Father Knows Best* or *I Remember Mama* series," Marshall explained to me. "I didn't want to. I didn't live in the 1930's. I said I would do it, though, if I could set the series in the 1950's instead of the 1930's. I grew up in the 1950's. I went through high school, college, and into the Army during that time. I know something about the '50's!"

Miller wasn't about to give up. He went back to Eisner at ABC and told him Marshall would take the job if he could move the time up 20 years. Eisner agreed. Marshall went to work on a script.

When he was finished, Miller and his partner, Edward K. Milkis, filmed the show. In it, they put three people we know today. Ron Howard played Richard Cunningham, Anson Williams was Richie's friend Potsie Weber, and Marion Ross was his mother.

The character of Fonzie wasn't in this

original version. And the show didn't sell. Somehow, despite all the high hopes and hard work, it just didn't turn out as well as expected. "It was good," Miller recalled, "but maybe it was too 'warm.' The people were all about the same with their middle-class virtues and goals. The network began to think that maybe the 1950's wouldn't be a popular time. So they put the film away without showing it."

Then, a year later, the movie *American Graffiti* came out. It was the story of teenagers in the early 1960's — and it was a tremendous success!

"We were later accused of copying *American Graffiti*," Miller noted. "That wasn't true at all. Our film had already been done and put away. The producers of *American Graffiti* called us and asked to see it, in fact. They wanted to see Ron Howard's performance in our show before they cast him in *American Graffiti*."

So *American Graffiti* got all the attention — and the *Happy Days* film sat on the shelf gathering dust.

And then one day Miller and Eisner got together again. "Almost two years had passed since we'd done the film of *Happy*

Days," Miller recalled. "And the subject came up again. Eisner said we should take another try at it. 'Do another script,' he said. Garry Marshall agreed to write a new script."

This time, Marshall drew more heavily on his own background. He thought about real kids he'd known when he was growing up in New York. And he added a character who would be slightly different from Richie Cunningham and the others — a cool character "from the other side of the tracks." He added Arthur Fonzarelli.

Miller and Milkis took it from there. "We spent weeks casting the show," Miller explained. "We saw hundreds and hundreds of kids. We wanted to get the best possible people in case the network decided to make a series of it. Ron Howard and Anson Williams were still the best around for the parts of Richie and Potsie. Our only concern was that they were several years older than they'd been when we'd made the original film. But after all the people we went through, they and Marion Ross were still the best. The network saw it, too."

Fine. But what about Fonzie? "We couldn't find him," Miller admitted. "We looked and looked. We had everybody else pretty much locked in. Donny Most tested for the part of Potsie. We liked him, so we gave him the Ralph Malph part. We didn't have Joanie until we saw Erin Moran on a TV show several nights before we were to go into production.

"But we still couldn't find Fonzie — and we were ready to start filming the show. Our Fonzie, as written, was like a 6′2″ hulking guy — the stereotyped big blond athlete. We saw hundreds of guys and nobody was right! Finally the casting director said, 'Hey, there's a young man here from New York who had a line on *The Mary Tyler Moore Show*.' We agreed to see him."

Time was running out. "And then," Miller said with a smile, "in walked Henry Winkler. He was not tall or large. He needed a shave. He was carrying a kind of green tote bag. He said, 'I apologize. I'm not right for this part.' He was so nice, so polite, so intelligent, so bright. We said, 'Will you read?' He said, 'Yes.' "

Tom Miller will never forget what happened next. Such moments do not happen often.

"Henry turned away to put down his

tote bag," Miller said. "Then he turned back, and suddenly, he was Fonzie. It was incredible. He was absolutely immersed in the character.

"He had only four lines in the script — and he was absolutely brilliant. He was exactly the opposite image of what we'd all expected. We called Garry Marshall and said, 'We've found him, but he's not what we expected.' Garry trusted us. He said, 'Fine — let's go with him.'

"The next morning," Miller said, "I got a call. 'Henry doesn't want to do it,' his agent said." Miller's heart dropped. Henry didn't want to play Fonzie?

"Look," his agent explained, "he's just out from New York. You only want him for seven out of 13 shows."

"I said we'd make it 11 out of 13 shows," Miller said. "His agent said, 'He only has four lines.' I said we'd make it more!" Finally Henry's agent told Miller that Henry was home. She suggested Miller call him.

Miller smiled at the memory. We all like to remember the times when we made the *right* decision. Miller had decided that he wanted Henry Winkler at all costs — and that was probably one of the smartest decisions of his entire career.

"I called Henry," Miller told me. "Little did I know how important that call would be — for all of us. Henry was *very* polite. He called me, 'Mr. Miller,' not Tom." Miller laughed. The producer is a young, friendly, outgoing person. People just naturally call him Tom.

"I finally said, 'Hey, my name is Tom.' Henry said, 'Yes, sir, Tom.' Miller grinned. "Henry was very honest, very direct. He said, 'If the role is so important, why do you want me only in seven out of 13 shows?' Henry wasn't asking for star billing," Miller hastened to add. "He just wanted to make sure he wasn't locking himself into an unimportant role.

"I told Henry we thought he was extraordinarily talented. I asked him to trust us. He believed me. He said, 'Let me think about it.' The topper was that I had to tell him that if he took the part, he'd have to come back and read for the head of the network." Miller is well aware that many performers are very temperamental. But not Henry Winkler.

"He said, 'Sure, I'll read again.' His feeling was that, 'If they don't want me, I don't want the job.' "

Miller looked around the office where we were sitting. It was a large, comfortable, cheerful room. "Henry came in and read in this office," he said. "I told the head of the network, 'This guy is going to be a star.' The network executive replied, 'Well, he's not going to be a star but he's okay.' " He's "okay"? That was probably the understatement of the year!

The network was very concerned that Fonzie would be a hood, Miller told me. "They just didn't see how great Henry is," Miller added.

"The very first day of shooting we were at a drive-in out in the Valley and I heard someone yell, 'Call from so-and-so at ABC.' I went across to a gas station and called him back. He said, 'How's his hair?' meaning Fonzie's. I yelled, YOU'RE CALLING ME TO FIND OUT HOW HIS HAIR IS? I couldn't believe it! The network also wanted to see the film we shot every day. They were very nervous. They didn't want Fonzie to be a hood."

The network may have been nervous, but audiences loved Fonzie from the very beginning.

Henry Studied Hard To Play a High School Dropout

The first time I met Henry Winkler, on that cold day in 1974, he had been playing Fonzie for some time. But Fonzie hadn't moved to the Cunninghams — and he hadn't become the gigantic star that he is today.

Henry admitted then that he was surprised when he got the part of Fonzie. "They wanted a big guy with greasy hair," he told me. "When I walked in, I said, 'Excuse me. I don't think I'm the guy you want.' But they put me on a motorcycle. They showed me where the camera would be. And they gave me lines to say. I made up the character as I went along."

"Fonzie is a tough guy who acts cool, but I wanted him to be a human being. I wanted him to be someone who makes mistakes. I refused to have him combing his hair all the time. Fonzie may have a soul of leather but he has a big heart!"

Henry was born in New York City. He is the only son of Ilse and Harry Winkler, who is president of an international lumber corporation. Both of Henry's parents were born in Germany. Both of them wanted and expected their son to become a successful businessman. He would follow in his father's footsteps, they believed, and be a credit to the family name.

But from the time he was seven years old, Henry wanted to be an actor. He made his acting debut at the Hilltop Nursery School. He played a tube of toothpaste and "recreated the part in first grade." He played the role of Billy Budd in the eighth grade and appeared in his first musical, *Of Thee I Sing*, while in the 11th grade.

His parents were horrified at this turn of events. They weren't at all happy about his acting ambitions, and they let him know it at every opportunity. "My parents were very much against my becoming an actor," Henry recalled. "They kept me out of everything they could."

Henry was very sensitive as a child. "I

cried myself to sleep many nights," he admitted. He knew his father was working hard to give him the best of everything — but their dreams just weren't the same. He tried sneaking out to auditions for plays, but he usually got caught.

He lived with his parents and older sister in a good neighborhood on the West Side of New York. "I was sent to private high school, where I wore blue blazers and gray slacks," he remembered.

"I was a terrible student in high school. I took geometry — the same course — for four years. I was told I was smart, but I was rebelling. I did much better in college, where I studied drama. I did better because I was working for myself, not for anybody else."

During high school and college, Henry studied in Switzerland for four-month intervals and worked in a lumber mill in a small German town. Nothing sidetracked him from his acting ambitions, however. He was graduated from McBurney School for Boys in New York City and then went to Emerson College in Boston, where he studied drama and psychology. He later spent a year and a half at Yale as a professional member of the university theater group. While there, he performed in more than 30 plays.

"I trained for nine years to become an actor," Henry declared. Fonzie is a high school dropout. "But I did not become a dropout by dropping out!" Henry said. "I went to school. I have a master's degree in theater arts."

"One thing I learned in drama school," Henry confided. "Don't live in the middle. Be committed to your life and to yourself. Be in a situation because you *want* to be there."

Henry was never convinced he could make it, but he was sure going to try. "I was not put on this earth for you, or you for me," he stressed. "I was put on this earth for *me*."

Doubts continually plagued him. "In college I knew I wasn't good enough," he told one friend. "When I auditioned for Yale to get my master's degree in drama, I knew I wasn't going to be accepted. The first day at Yale they told us, 'A lot of you aren't going to make it.' I packed my bags."

He needn't have bothered. He was accepted and he made it through. He learned a great deal. "The theater is so important!" he said. "It juices you up! The stage is where you learn to act!"

Having learned, Henry knew where he had to head next. Home to New York. He rented an apartment and struck out on his own. He pursued his acting career by doing a number of radio and TV commercials and by appearing in plays, on and off Broadway.

"The commercials helped me learn how to work in front of a camera," he told a New York reporter. "Up to then, all my experience had been on stage, which is vital to any actor. I did those commercials as seriously as I did Shakespeare in college."

Henry was keeping busy in New York, but his agent thought he should try Hollywood. "I'd done two movies, 30 commercials, and so on," Henry reminisced. "I thought I was doing all right." But he followed his agent's advice and moved to California on September 20, 1973. He had $1,000 and had decided he would stay for one month. He knew one person — a girl he had met in college.

It didn't take him long to discover that his agent had been right to send him to California, where most TV shows are produced. He was able to obtain several auditions. "I arrived on September 20. On October 5, I started working on a segment of *The Mary Tyler Moore Show*," Henry recalled. Henry also appeared on *The Bob Newhart Show* and did a CBS movie, *Menace*, with Patty Duke.

"I got the role of Fonzie on my birthday, October 30," he said.

On this first time we met, Henry and I had lunch at Alfredo's in New York. Henry had come home for the holidays — and he had been having a great time. Even his parents were no longer opposed to their son's being an actor!

"The 1950's seemed to be a time when many people lived comfortably," Henry pointed out. "But it also seemed to be a boring, uninformed time. Our show is a romantic look at the past. Young people like it because they can see how their parents lived. They like the music of the 50's.

"Young people also seem to like the character of Fonzie," Henry said. "I must sign 50 autographs a day. The last time I was in New York, I was stopped about every 20 seconds.

"For four years I have been self-sufficient as an actor. I'm actually very lucky, aren't I?" Being famous is fun, Henry admitted. "But the main thing is that I'm doing what I want to do. I've worked hard. I didn't want to act if I couldn't do it well. It's not easy getting acting jobs. I have to know what I'm doing.

"*Happy Days* is a half hour of hassle-free time. It's entertainment. I can't make it more than it is. One reason entertainment exists is to show life at a heightened level. The relationships on *Happy Days* could happen in real life. The relationship between Richie Cunningham and his father is very important. On the show father is not always right.

"Such relationships seldom exist in real life," Henry added, "because of our lack of respect for ourselves. The little ways I command respect come from my respect for myself. I stand up for myself. I stand up for Fonzie.

"Acting is an art. I could get sloppy. That's why I do so much homework. There have been times when I didn't do my homework and it showed. Every night while the show was in production I would go home and study the script. I would ask myself: What was Fonzie saying? Why was he saying it? What was his motivation? Was it the right thing for him to say?"

Henry has tried hard not to let the public acclaim go to his head. "I love applause but if you ever dare to believe that it's real, it's all over," he said. "You have to keep your feet on the ground.

"One way I relax is to dance. I love dancing. I dance out my anger. I dance until I fall down! I use music to create. I do rock and roll, modern jazz, many things.

"Sometimes I also go to a juvenile hall in Los Angeles. I love kids. I just visit with them. We talk about the show and about everything. I enjoy that."

Our luncheon was drawing to a close. Henry and I donned our heavy winter coats and walked out into the chill wintry afternoon. It would be five months before I'd see Henry again. Many things would happen to him before then.

"Heyyyy"— It Worked!

When Garry Marshall created the character of Fonzie, he was trying to create a new kind of television hero. "We felt that young people needed a more traditional kind of hero than a David Cassidy or *The Brady Bunch*," Marshall told me. "We were trying to create a certain kind of hero who would fit into the 1970's. We had to set the show in the 1950's to make it work. So many people are heroes because they are good-looking. We wanted a hero who did things.

"The character of Fonzie offers a good philosophy for young people: 'You can make it despite all odds.' That sounds pretentious, but I believe it. Somebody should make a positive statement and that's what we're trying to do."

At one point, the producers of *Happy*

Days almost called the show *Cool*, Marshall said. "But we were afraid people would think it was a show about Eskimos," he laughed. "So we ended up calling it *Happy Days*, though nobody was very crazy about that title."

Marshall based the character of Fonzie on three people — himself "and two guys I grew up with in New York," he said. "One of those guys was a very, very tough guy. He was much meaner than Fonzie. He's probably in jail now. But despite his toughness, he had tremendous love of God, country, mother, father, his elders, and so on. I used that combination of qualities in the character of Fonzie. Fonzie respects all those things. He doesn't fool around with them.

"I still see a little of myself in Fonzie," Marshall added. "Henry Winkler's background is not at all like Fonzie's. Henry hadn't the slightest idea how to ride a motorcycle. He'd never been on one in his life. He spent hours learning to drive the thing. The first time he drove it he almost wiped out the camera crew!

"Fonzie, with all his stuff, has never done anything he was ashamed of," Marshall pointed out. "Maybe he's not what you'd call a 'good boy,' but he's not robbed or beaten people just for the sake of beating them up.

"Fonzie doesn't smoke because smoking could hurt you. Why hurt yourself? That's Fonzie's attitude. He drinks beer, but heavy drinking isn't cool. He only does things that are cool. He doesn't make a big show of it. It's just the way he is. Smoking isn't cool, wearing glasses is. It's not deep philosophy. It's just something that's there."

Marshall created Fonzie on paper. Henry Winkler created him on film. "We set the characters in general," Marshall explained. "But all actors change their characters somewhat by using certain gestures and so on. We gave Fonzie, 'Hey,' but Henry made it his own. We gave him the thumbs-up gesture — he made a life of that thumbs-up gesture!"

Marshall smiled. To everyone involved, it is a joy when a character clicks. It takes the right combination of talents behind the scenes — and superb acting on camera.

"Fonzie doesn't talk down to kids," Marshall noted. "Kids believe him. Henry's philosophy in life is similar to mine. He feels, as I do, that if you want to do something in life you must do it. Even if others make fun of you — if you enjoy doing something, don't pay attention to them. This is not necessarily 'do your own thing,' but 'be your own person.' "

Marshall comes up with many of the ideas for the *Happy Days* shows. "I try to remember things I did as a kid," he said. "When we have writers' meetings, we don't discuss *ideas* so much as *incidents* in our lives. People think that ideas come from imagination. Actually, experience is one of the best places to get ideas. We sit in writers' meetings and talk about being young. We talk about things that happened to us. One of us might say, 'Once when I was 14 I had a fight with a bully...' Often we come up with story ideas from such memories."

Putting a show together isn't easy, Marshall admitted. "Somebody creates characters. Writers work on ideas for scripts. All of it takes time. Once we have the script, Miller and Milkis do the production work. They do the casting, editing, music, and so on. On *Happy Days*, it takes 78 people, including the actors, to make one episode. When we're filming the show, at least 50 people are usually working together on the stage, on camera and off."

When Marshall remembers his own high school days, he is remembering DeWitt Clinton High School in New York. "High school was not especially painful for me," he said, "but the times that were nice were not especially humorous. To the writers I say, 'Tell me a time when you *lost*.' I think the boy-girl relationship is always a big thing with young people. I don't think any boy was ever born knowing how to handle girls — or girls born knowing how to handle boys. Those are things you have to learn.

"I think one of the worst things about being young is the feeling of being isolated and alone. A young person thinks, 'I'm the only one with this problem.' One thing we're trying to say in *Happy Days* is, 'You're *not* alone. You're not the only one with problems.' We can't solve anyone's problems, but we can show them that they're not weird for having problems!

"That's one thing we've tried to get across in the show, through all the characters — that it's painful to grow up. We make a comedy out of it — but young viewers know someone else has been there," Marshall stressed.

When *Happy Days* started, Marshall said, "We were aiming for a show that all the kids would watch, and a show that their parents wouldn't find boring. So many young people's shows put their parents to sleep," he added with a smile. "By setting *Happy Days* in the 1950's, it gives parents a chance to think about their own lives during that time — and to tell their children about their lives. At first," Marshall acknowledged, "only kids were into the show. Gradually, we began to get the parents. To be one of the top shows, you have to get viewers of all ages. Now we find that everyone in the family is enjoying *Happy Days*."

That's true now. But in the beginning, as Marshall admitted, it was young people who kept the show alive. *Happy Days* premiered on ABC in January of 1974. Here is how the network described the show at that time:

"The series centers around two high school students, innocent Richie Cunningham, played by Ron Howard, and his worldlier friend, Potsie Weber, who are growing up in the era when rock 'n' roll was rampant and Uncle Miltie was the kingpin of television. Richie's relationships with the members of his family and his activities with his friends are revealing of the relatively carefree life and lifestyles of young people in those bygone, happy, innocent days.

"Co-starring in the series are Tom Bosley as Richie's father; Marion Ross as Marion Cunningham, Richie's mother; Anson Williams as his pal, Potsie; Henry Winkler as Fonzie, a motorcycle buff; and Donny Most, as Ralph Malph."

The names of the actors and the characters are the same now as they were then. But major changes have been made in the series since it first went on the air. Producer Tom Miller explained why.

"The series was very successful when it premiered opposite *Maude* and *Adam-12*," he told me. "Both those shows were in the Top 10. They weren't concerned about *Happy Days* — and *Happy Days* started out like gang busters. Then the second year we got clobbered by *Good Times*. I think everybody decided *Happy Days* had gotten too soft, that it needed stronger characters. *Good Times* had a slightly harder edge. At that time, CBS also had a comedy block of *Good Times* and *M*A*S*H.* We were getting killed. So Michael Eisner at ABC said, 'I won't move it away from *Good Times.* But if we go three-camera live in front of an audience, and put a little more emphasis on Fonzie, I think we can make the show better.' "

It was clear to everybody that changes had to be made or the show would be canceled. Up until then, the show had been filmed in bits and pieces without an audience. Eisner was suggesting that they film a live performance being done before an audience. They didn't have much time to try the idea. "We were about finished filming for the season," Miller recalled. "Eisner even had the idea for the show, though. In it, Fonzie got engaged to a girl who turned out to be a stripper. What the network wanted was to make *Happy Days* not just the story of Richie Cunningham growing up in the 1950's, but Richie and his friend Fonzie growing up."

They tried the idea and it worked. "We filmed the show before a live audience and it tested very well," Miller said. "The series was picked up for another season. From then on, we've done it before an audience, and that makes a big difference. It's hard not to be funny when there is an audience sitting right there!

"Garry Marshall came up with the brilliant idea of moving Fonzie to the Cunninghams'. That way we could make Fonzie prominent along with Richie."

Great. But what would Ron Howard, who plays Richie, say about such a move? He was, in effect, being asked to share the starring role. Many performers would never go along with such a plan. They would be concerned, not about what was best for the show, but what was best for them.

Ron Howard is young, but he is a veteran actor. And he is quite a person. *Happy Days*' three executive producers—Marshall, Miller, and Milkis—went to see him. "He was fantastic," Miller revealed. "He said, 'I want what is best for the show.' We told him we wanted to raise Henry Winkler to star status. We are a group—and no one knows that better than Ron Howard."

The changes were made. Like fireworks on the Fourth of July, the show's ratings skyrocketed. Fonzie became an even bigger star, but he didn't do it alone.

"Henry believes it's Ron Howard who allows Fonzie to soar," Miller added. "Henry feels that because Ron plays it so legit, so straight, it allows his character to go off and to have believability. Ron has to be one of the most gifted actors I've ever seen."

These Are Happy Days for Ron Howard

I had heard a great deal about Ron Howard before I met him in the summer of 1974. Ron is a veteran actor at the age of 22. He's been working regularly since he was four years old — yet he seems to have no ego problems or big-shot complexes. He is a pleasant, level-headed young man who has a great deal going for him.

I met Ron for lunch in the Paramount commissary. This is a cafeteria where all the performers, technicians, and others go for lunch on days when they are working. You see actors and actresses dressed in all kinds of costumes, depending on what movies or TV shows are being filmed at the time. The day I met Ron, I followed a man who looked like Abraham Lincoln through the cafeteria line. The actor would eat his lunch quickly and then get back to work.

Ron was busy working on *Happy Days*. The show had come on in January as a mid-season replacement. It's never easy for a show to come on in the middle of the year, but *Happy Days* had done well enough to be renewed for another season.

Ron grew up on television. But despite all the fame and the attention he has received, he has managed to keep his feet on the ground. He gives his parents credit for that. His parents knew show business — and they didn't want a swell-headed kid in their midst. They considered acting a good way of making a living and that was all.

Ron was born in Duncan, Oklahoma. His father, Rance, is a character actor who's been in a number of Westerns. Ron's mother, Jean, was an actress who gave up her career when Ron and his younger brother came along. Rance and Jean met at the University of Oklahoma when they were cast in a play together.

Ron went on stage for the first time when he was two. His parents were doing *The Seven Year Itch* in Baltimore and Ron made a brief appearance. He didn't get paid for it, though, so he says he really made his professional debut when he was four. That was in the movie *The Journey* with Yul Brynner and Deborah Kerr.

Producer Sheldon Leonard saw Ron in a *G.E. Theatre* production and cast him as Andy Griffith's son Opie in *The Andy Griffith Show*. Ron was six years old at the time.

"I was in that series until I was 14," Ron recalled. "I've always enjoyed working. If I hadn't enjoyed it, I wouldn't have done it — and my parents wouldn't have let me. That would have been destructive. I always had the option of turning work down."

He didn't turn much of it down, though. Even while he was on *The Andy Griffith Show* he found time to be in movies and other TV shows. When he wasn't working, he found he missed it. "That's when I knew for sure that I wanted to be in this business," he said.

After Andy's show was canceled, Ron appeared in segments of a number of TV shows, including *The FBI*, *Daniel Boone*, *Gentle Ben*, and *Gunsmoke*. He also starred in the Disney movie, *Wild Country*, with his brother Clint, and co-starred in *The Smith Family* series on ABC.

Then along came the movie *American Graffiti*, a smash hit at the box office. In it Ron played a high school senior in the early 1960's.

Now he's playing a similar role in *Happy Days* — and Ron doesn't mind at all being typecast as a high school student of 20 years ago. "I can relate to those days," he said. "I'm not convinced the 1950's were much different from the late 1960's and early 1970's when I was in high school. The problems are basically the same — first cars, dating, getting a job, trying to do well in school."

Ron paused and thought for a minute. He was remembering his own high school days. He had been graduated from a high school in Burbank, California, in 1972. "I don't believe the *group* was as important when I was in high school, nor was the family," he continued. "It was more of an individual effort. Group pressure did exist, but it didn't carry the power that it seems to have carried in the 1950's. I've tried to find out about that period. I looked through magazines and yearbooks of the 1950's. And when people come up to me and say, 'That's my era!' I ask them about it. *Happy Days* has a staff of people who make sure we use the right expressions, wear the right clothes, drive the right model cars, and so on."

During his own high school days, Ron was an avid baseball and basketball player. Sports, he found, were a great equalizer. "At first it was a big novelty that I was an actor, but the fact that I was good in athletics helped people accept me," he said. "They realized that I was just a person who happened to do this other thing, acting, on the side. Sports were the common ground. That's even been shown on a worldwide level where athletics have become a diplomatic tool."

Ron played on the school basketball team for two years and in the park and recreation league. When I met him in 1974, he was coaching a team of 13-to-15-year-olds. "It's a baseball team in the Senior League — an offshoot of the Little League," he explained to me. At that time, he said, he was spending nine to 10 hours a week with the team, on weekends and at night.

Ron started college at the University of Southern California, but he had to drop out when *Happy Days* came along. He hopes to continue his education, he said, by going to school at night. "I'd like to major in cinema arts. Education is very important. I may not be able to get my degree, but I feel I need that scholastic experience to round me out."

Ron worked much of the time while he was growing up, but he still had to help around the house. "My brother and I had responsibilities, but our household never ran as smoothly as others. We spent more time together than many families. When my father wasn't working, he'd be at home. We did many things together, though we didn't travel a lot. When you're a free-lance actor like my dad, you can't afford to miss a job.

"I owe my dad an awful lot," Ron admitted. "He helped me a great deal with my acting; then he took time to come to the set when I was working and help me understand what the director wanted of me. I'm always interested in watching other people's acting techniques — and here again my father has been tremendously influential. That's one reason why I think I did well in this industry as a kid. Having someone like Dad who knows the industry and who will work with you is invaluable."

It was his parents, Ron said, who have helped him keep his career in perspective. "They believed in simplicity to the hilt," he explained. "I think that's why they've been so successful. If parents get carried away, a kid will too. If parents have a good attitude toward the business, they can help a kid keep things in perspective.

"If you don't watch it, things can be blown all out of proportion. You find yourself believing things you shouldn't believe. You start misinterpreting and getting generally crazy because people react to you in such strange ways. You have to be aware of that, or it becomes more than an actor acting. People outside the business make such a big deal of those in the business that you begin to think, 'Yes, maybe we are terrific!'

"My brother and I both got in this business very early. We learned quickly that it's an exciting, terrific way to make a living. I don't think anyone should believe that the industry is all glamor, though."

I asked Ron why he thought a show like *Happy Days* was doing well. "I think people were ready for a show of this kind," he replied. "We deal with happy days, not with the problems of the 1950's. We call back times that people remember as being pleasant. I think *The Mary Tyler Moore Show* has the same basic approach to modern-day subjects."

Ron has been acting almost all his life and he's not tired of it yet. "It's hard work, but if you like something, you give it all you've got," he said enthusiastically. "An athlete doesn't come in from a ball game and say, 'Gee, I raced through that.' No, it isn't easy, but if you like it you want to do it well. I can't think of much I don't like about it. It's a terrific way to make a living."

Ron had told me all this during our luncheon in the summer of 1974. Almost two years passed before I talked to him again. By then, changes had been made — in *Happy Days* and in his life. I asked him what he thought of the changes that had been made in *Happy Days*.

"Making the switch to a three-camera show has really helped the writers and the actors," he replied enthusiastically. "Having an audience is invaluable. It spurs you on. You're up for every scene. When you're doing a one-camera show, a certain number of scenes are shot at the end of the day when you're dragged out. Now we rehearse all week and film the show on Friday. That means we can change and improve until the very last minute."

What about moving Fonzie to the Cunninghams' and giving him a bigger part in the show? "It was a step the network wanted to take and the producers were willing to try it," Ron explained. "It has worked out beautifully. It was an adjustment I had to make. It was an action I believe was right. Had I been producing the show, I would have gone for more balance — and that's what this has done."

"During the first two years of the show, 80 percent of the stories revolved around my character, Richie Cunningham. They were about the problems Richie got into. This past year, there was better balance. Some of the shows centered on Richie's problems, some centered on Fonzie's, some centered on Potsie's and Ralph's. I think that has helped. At first I wasn't sure it would be good for everybody, but it was a decision that was made. Richie still plays a strong role. The stories are still told from his point of view and he's in on all the solutions to the problems. Really, it was not as drastic a change as it might seem."

Happy Days was out of production when I last talked to Ron. But as usual, he was busy working. "I've been doing a movie with John Wayne and Lauren Bacall," he told me. "It's been a fantastic experience! It's called *The Shootist.* I play Lauren Bacall's son. She's a widow who owns a boarding house. John Wayne comes to town and finds he's dying of cancer. He's a famous shootist — a famous gunfighter. He takes on sort of a father image to me. It's set at the turn of the century, when the West was really dying out."

Ron married his long-time girlfriend, Cheryl Alley, on June 7, 1975. "She's a psychology major," he said proudly. "We enjoy doing many things. We go to a lot of movies. We live in an apartment in Los Angeles."

Ron hasn't had time to go back to school himself or to coach young baseball players. "I'm working on a film project," he explained. "My father and I wrote a film we're trying to get produced. Then I'd like to direct it. I'm also producing and directing a 16mm film project."

Ron hopes very much to be a director some day. "Writing, too, has become more of an interest to me," he said. "A director has to be able to write. Half of making a film is rewriting and restructuring — that's why writing is so important. Also it would seem to me that it would be much easier to make a film you've written and understand than trying to take someone else's film and make it work for you."

These are happy days — in more ways than one! — for Ron. "People at *Happy Days* have been extremely cooperative with me," he noted. "I made a crazy little film called *Eat My Dust*! at the same time we were doing *Happy Days*. They worked around me so I could do the film. Not that many people have a chance to do both films and TV. I feel very lucky. I'm in a good frame of mind."

"Are you getting tired of playing Richie Cunningham?" I asked Ron.

"This is my third TV series," he replied. "Any time you do a TV series you get a little tired of it. It's bound to get repetitious. Stories and jokes repeat themselves. But doing the show in front of an audience helps. I'd never worked in front of an audience before.

"There's no doubt the shows have gotten better. We fell into a very comfortable format last year. We're no longer floundering around."

Ron himself has never floundered around. He has been acting for 18 of his 22 years. He is a happy, talented young man who has kept his career in orbit and his feet on the ground.

The producers of *Happy Days* weren't really surprised at his reaction when they went to see him about changes in the show. Ron Howard has never been one to let his ego stand in the way of his good sense. Would *Happy Days* be a better, stronger show if Fonzie had a bigger part? If so, Ron agreed, move him closer to the scene of much of the action. There was room for Fonzie at the Cunninghams' home.

FONZIE'S
HAPPY DAYS
ALBUM

Ironing is for nerds? Don't tell that to the Fonz! He's become the coolest character on TV.

It takes two to make a super team—and Richie Cunningham (Ron Howard) and Arthur Fonzarelli (Henry Winkler) have become just that. They make each other look good. "Ron's acting is so good it allows me to soar," says Henry.

Producer Garry Marshall wanted to create the kind of hero who did many things. Fonzie is that kind of hero. He even jumped over a row of garbage cans on his motorcycle. But then he decided that the Fonz should have known better. It wasn't really a cool thing to do.

Joanie Cunningham (Erin Moran) is growing up and it isn't always easy. She has a big crush on Potsie. But to him, she's just Richie's little sister. Can the Fonz help? He'll surely try. Sometimes his ideas even work!

Henry didn't think he was right for the role of the Fonz. He created the character as he went along. Fortunately, it wasn't all just hard work, as you can see here. Merry Christmas!

The Cunninghams have become the family Fonzie never had. Does Mr. Cunningham (Tom Bosley) object to a dance contest? It looks like it! Mrs. Cunningham (Marion Ross) doesn't agree.

Who needs Elvis Presley? The Fonz will save the big senior dance! The chorus girls went on to a hit TV show of their own. Laverne and Shirley first appeared on *Happy Days*. In real life, they're Penny Marshall and Cindy Williams.

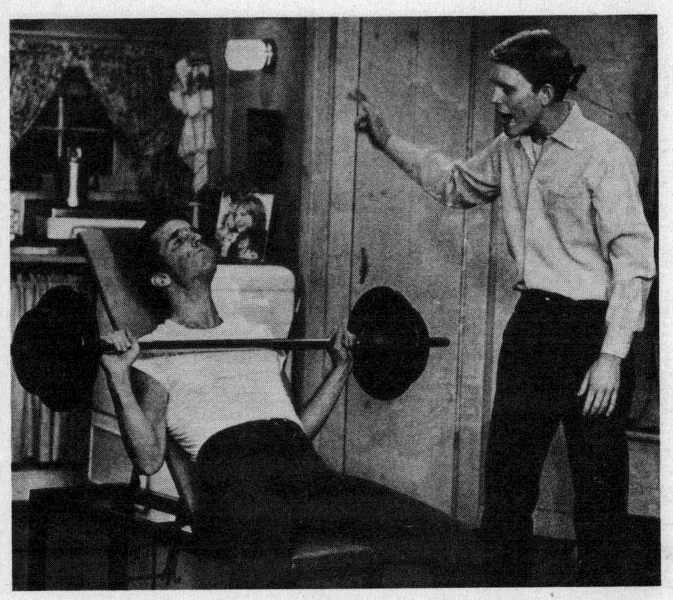

"You've got to listen to me, Fonzie!" Richie begs. But he's getting the strong, silent act from the muscle-building Fonzie. One... two...

Richie Cunningham (Ron Howard) is tired of being humiliated by bullies. He's taking jujitsu lessons from Arnold (Pat Morita).

Mrs. Cunningham (Marion Ross) has special privileges. She's allowed to call Fonzie by his real name of Arthur—and she's permitted to give him a kiss on the cheek. Legions of fans would like to do the same!

In her dreams, Joanie (Erin Moran) is seeing her wedding—to Potsie (Anson Williams), of course! Fonzie got all dressed up for the wedding in "They Call It Potsie Love." And Joanie got *almost* all dressed in bridal garb.

Fonzie—"the tough guy"—visits his friends in jail. "It was this way, Your Honor: They broke the Curfew. It was a bad night in Milwaukee."

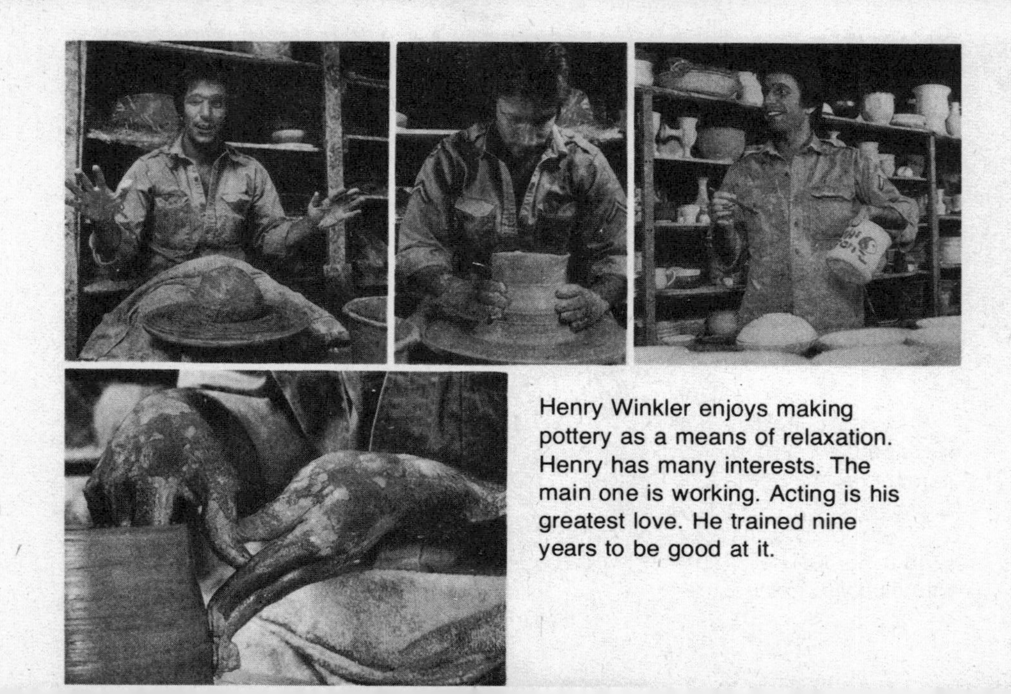

Henry Winkler enjoys making pottery as a means of relaxation. Henry has many interests. The main one is working. Acting is his greatest love. He trained nine years to be good at it.

Moments of relaxation are rare for Henry these days. He is swamped with requests for interviews, autographs, and personal appearances. Free time is to be enjoyed to the fullest.

They're growing up in the 1950's and we're sharing the fun with them. From the top left: Ron Howard (Ritchie), Anson Williams (Potsie), Donny Most (Ralph) and Henry Winkler (Fonzie). They've made *Happy Days* a happy place to be. They give it their all!

Would the Fans Like Him?
Henry Winkler Wasn't Sure

Henry Winkler was the first one who told me, when I saw him in May of 1975, that Fonzie would be moving to the Cunninghams' the following season. He didn't know then, and neither did anyone else, how important that move would be.

Henry only knew that the show had been out of production for some months. And one thing makes Henry very unhappy. That's not working.

I hadn't seen Henry for five months. It had been cold and wintry in New York then. Now it was warm and sunny in Los Angeles. Henry looked different. His hair was longer and he'd grown a mustache. I asked him what he'd been doing since I'd seen him last.

"I did three talk shows," he told me. "I made my dancing debut on Merv Griffin's show! Then I went to Milwaukee to do a telethon for epilepsy — and 70,000 people showed up to say hello! After that I read for a part in a film but I didn't get it. So I took a trip with friends up the California coast. I'd never seen Carmel — it was one of the most spectacular sights of my life."

The lack of work was getting to him, however. "The thing I most enjoy is working," he exclaimed. "I trained nine years and I don't want to sit. I want to work. I don't think I *deserve* work — I just want a whack at it. I have been given four movie scripts. Three I turned down because of the scripts; one I turned down because the director was a sham."

The life of an actor is always an uncertain one. Henry knows that. The public is fickle. They may love you today and forget you tomorrow. Or you may be a huge hit with the public — and still have Hollywood producers ignore you when it comes to casting a new show. Henry, as Fonzie, is enormously popular with TV viewers. But TV shows aren't in production year-round. There are many months of the year when Henry isn't playing Fonzie. It is those months he wants to fill.

As I listened to Henry describe his dreams and his discouragements, I realized that this second meeting was much different from our first. We were no longer strangers. Henry was calmer. He was more open and direct. He's like most of us — he moves slowly when he meets a new person. He will be friendly and polite — but friendship is something that has to grow over a period of time.

"I'm often discouraged," Henry admitted. "Anxiety and discouragement and the feeling that I'll never work again so long as I live are everyday occurrences. I think there's a voice in every actor saying, 'I want you to fail.' I believe that's universal.

"People think they are doing you a service by giving you *words*. They tell you who you are. They say, 'You're a star!' 'You're the best!' It's so out of proportion. You start to believe it! Then you say, 'But if I'm so good, I should be working!' You find you may be popular but many people haven't heard of you — or a producer may have heard of you and think of you just as a comedy actor. But," Henry added philosophically, "it will come to me."

His moments of discouragement, he's

found, always pass. "I have learned that no matter how discouraged I am I'll get over it," Henry said. "I've gone through identity crises. Sure, it's difficult to be insecure and out of work, but it will change. I know it will."

Things were already looking up for him, in fact. He had just had an exciting few days. "I went to Hawaii to do an Easter Seals telethon," he said. "It was a fabulous experience! The first night I was taken out to dinner by 20 women from the front desk of the hotel where I was staying. *Happy Days* does fabulously well in Hawaii. It seemed like everybody around came to say hello. I loved it there. It was very calm and relaxed. I got to meet Rosemary Clooney and Jessica Walter, who were also working on the telethon.

"Then I came back here and the last 72 hours have been very exciting. Sunday afternoon I got a knock at the door. A guy said, 'Have you seen your car lately?' I ran down to the garage where I keep it. Someone had introduced my car to a sledgehammer and stolen the stereo tape deck.

"That same night," Henry continued, "I was a presenter on the local Emmy awards show. That was the first time I'd done that — and I love 'firsts.' Monday afternoon I found I had gotten my first part in a two-hour movie for ABC called *Katherine*. It's about an American terrorist in the 1960's.

"Tuesday afternoon I got a call from my insurance agent telling me to replace the tape deck. So I went out and bought one and had my car fixed! The point of all this," Henry explained, "is that I waited six months and then everything happened in two days, good *and* bad. All the energy I put out came back."

Henry began acting when he was a child. Through the years, he has played many roles and worked with many people. I asked him if any one person had been of special help to him. "There wasn't any one person, there were many," he replied. "Paula Prentiss, an actress friend of mine, once said to me: 'If you make it, you make it on your own.' I don't really believe that. Naturally you must deliver the goods when you're called on. But many people help you along the way. My theatrical agent helped. My music teacher in high school helped. My acting teacher was fabulous. He kicked me around for two years saying, 'Get busy. Get to work.' I owe a lot to Tom Miller, one of the producers of *Happy Days*. He talked to me and believed in me."

Ron Howard was also helpful, Henry acknowledged. "Ron taught me the technicalities of TV," Henry said. "He's very patient. He's a terrific guy."

Henry was new to TV. He didn't know how audiences would react to him. "When I knew the series was going on the air, I wondered if I'd get any fan mail — or any fans!" he laughed. "I had no idea I would appeal to women! I appreciate all the fans. I read every letter I get. (He would soon not be able to keep up with reading all the fan mail, however.) I love my audiences very much."

He has had very few unpleasant experiences with his fans, Henry told me during our meeting in May, 1975. "I've only had a few unpleasant experiences during all this time," he said. "One guy wanted to pick a fight and so on. I enjoy most people. I don't give them power over me, though. If I depended on those people to verify my existence, I'd be giving them a power I have no say in.

"Sometimes I'm approached by strangers who tell me: 'If you don't give us your autograph we won't watch your show anymore.'" Henry smiled. "Most people aren't like that. Most people are wonderful."

Henry is a bachelor. "There are advantages to being single," he pointed out. "I know more about myself under pressure. So many people graduate from high school, get married, have children — and then realize there were alternatives. Somehow we have gotten the idea that marriage is a must."

Henry dated two girls in high school, he said. "Now I don't date more than three at a time," he joked. "My biggest dating problem in high school was one I still have. I wanted to settle down and be free at the same time. I do want very much to settle down and be free at the same time. I'm halfway there. I know intellectually that within structure comes freedom, but...

"Women say, 'I don't want anything.' Then they start complaining, 'Why didn't you call?'" Henry shook his head.

Henry has definite ideas about the kinds of women he likes — and doesn't like. "I'll tell you exactly," he declared. "I like someone who is intelligent enough to have her own life and protective enough to be in love with me. I like someone with a sense of humor and someone who is able to be direct without being defensive. The thing that turns me off is a girl who thinks she's more than she is, a girl who cops an attitude. You see girls carrying their expensive Gucci bags. If you ask me, many of them are 'Gucci-brained.' I'm first attracted by what I see, though that's relative. I really go for brains first — brains and wit."

Henry watches a lot of TV. "I watch it in three ways," he said. "Sometimes I turn off the sound and just watch the actors. Sometimes I watch it because it calms me down. Other times I watch it to be entertained."

The better I have gotten to know Henry, the more surprised I have been at one thing. Unlike most actors, and most people in general, he has a very solid understanding of who he is and what he believes. I would see that even more clearly the next time I met him. But on this occasion, I asked him if there had been any one event that had triggered this awareness of himself. "At this moment," he replied, "my recollection is of being a freshman in high school and walking down the street. Suddenly, it was as if a dome had been lifted from my brain. For the first time, I became aware of the fact that I existed in that space and time. It was a revelation to me."

On *Happy Days*, Henry plays a teenager in the 1950's. He is well aware that life is much different for teenagers today. "It's tougher to grow up today. Life is so fast," he said. "Children get too much information too soon. In some cultures, a 13-year-old girl is considered an adult!"

Henry hopes to make more movies. "And I'd like to direct when I know more," he said. "I'd also like to act until I die.

"When I'm not working I enjoy horseback riding, watching TV, going to movies, and listening to music. My stereo is a very important possession. I'm looking forward," he added, "to the changes that are being made on *Happy Days*. Fonzie is moving into the Cunninghams' garage, so he'll always be around."

Henry has had his moments of discouragement, but he's never let them get him down. He's been able to take the bad *and* the good — and it's a good thing, for the 1975-76 television season was fast approaching. For months, people behind-the-scenes had been discussing making changes in *Happy Days*. But finally, viewers would be able to *see* the changes and make their own judgments. The show would be filmed before an audience. Fonzie would move to the Cunninghams'. Henry Winkler's life would be turned upside down.

Anson Williams: "I'm Not a Potsie!"

Happy Days has changed the lives of everyone in it. A stage performer plays to an audience of hundreds. A television performer plays to an audience of millions. It is a heady sensation. Suddenly you're in demand for telethons, personal appearances, and TV talk shows. People know your name and your face. They stop you on the street. What you do with that fame depends on you — on your interests and your goals. Henry Winkler and Ron Howard are interested in acting and directing. Anson Williams' greatest love is music.

Anson plays Potsie Weber in *Happy Days* — and occasionally he sings on the show. "I don't want to sing too much on the show," Anson told me. "I can't perform as I do in real life because it doesn't fit the character of Potsie. I'm also not crazy about doing songs from the 1950's. That's why I'd just as soon keep the singing at a minimum. I wrote some special music for *Happy Days*, though, and that was fun. I wrote a Hawaiian song and a limbo number."

The character of Potsie has changed since *Happy Days* first came on the air, Anson pointed out. "Potsie used to be the real instigator," he laughed. "He was 15 pounds heavier. He's slicker now. His clothes fit. He's become an 'aw, shucks,' character. And he's very honest. He always bears the brunt of everything. He's become very nice and very naive. Ralph Malph has taken over the instigator part. The change," Anson added, "just kind of happened as the show settled down.

"I think the show is better now that we do it in front of an audience," the young actor said. "Doing it this way means the writers can rewrite until the last minute, so the scripts are better. It's like doing a play. There's spontaneity and magic with the people. We've also dropped the nostalgia bit. Now we're just depending on comedy. The show just happens to take place in the 1950's. That's better.

"I like playing Potsie, but it's like any job. Some days are terrific, others are boring. I'm pretty grateful for it, though. I hope I'll be able to host a TV variety show when I'm done with *Happy Days*."

Anson was relaxing in the sunshine the day I talked to him, but he hasn't had much free time lately. In addition to pursuing his acting and singing careers, he has been traveling throughout the country as Honorary National Chairman of Concerned Youth for Cerebral Palsy, making numerous appearances at statewide telethons and other fund-raising events.

"This is my second year as honorary chairman," Anson explained. "I don't have as much time to spend on it as I did, but I'm doing what I can. I'm starting to do a few concerts for them. We make more money from the concerts than we do from the telethons. I take out expenses, but everything else goes to cerebral palsy."

"My dad's best friend from World War II had a daughter who was born with cerebral palsy. That's how I got involved. So far, I've helped raise three million dollars. When I visit a town, I meet with the young people who are involved with Concerned Youth for Cerebral Palsy. It has been quite an experience. I have learned a great deal from all of them — from the kids. The problem now is that my own work is beginning to take more and more of my time."

Anson was born in Los Angeles, the only son of Rosalind and Haskell Heimlick. His father is a fine commercial artist and sculptor.

He grew up in Burbank, California, where his parents and younger sister still live. He started writing poems when he was very young. "It was my way of dealing with the pain that is part of everybody's adolescence," he remembered. "I still find it the most wonderful therapy in the world."

Surfing was another thing he loved. "Surfing is where I learned humanity," he told one writer. "Surfers are special people. If you aren't honest, they won't bother with you. They will reject you if you're not kind. There are five people vying for this one wave, and on the day when the other four let you have it, you know you're in."

Anson became interested in acting while attending junior college. He then enrolled as a drama major at California State College. "I was 20 when I started in music," he laughed. "I fell into acting. I'm not an actor! I've been fooling everyone for four years! Being an apprentice in summer stock was the first time I got paid for acting. I was so bad at building sets that they put me on the stage. That was in Wichita, Kansas. I auditioned here in Los Angeles and then drove to Wichita. I've been supporting myself with my acting and my music for about four years."

But before that, he had to put himself through school. He described the experience to a New York columnist: "It was that fillet of fish commercial that started me. It ran for three years. They didn't want me for that. They said I was too young. I begged them. I said I was $1,000 in debt, carrying 15 units in college, desperate.

"I got it. That made it possible for me to give up working as a janitor, grill cook, and shoe salesman. If anything will give you ambition, it's being a shoe salesman."

Since then, Anson has done a number of TV commercials. One of them was a milestone of sorts: He was the first young man to leap over a McDonald's burger stand counter in a tall white hat singing "You deserve a break today..."

Anson grew up in a non-show business

family. "But everything came together for me when I took a theater arts course to round out my college schedule. I discovered the magic that can happen between a performer and an audience, and I know there can't be a greater feeling than the one I get every time I'm on stage," he said.

In Wichita, Kansas, he appeared in summer stock productions of *The Music Man*, *The Sound of Music*, and *South Pacific*. "I paid my dues in music," Anson told me. "Being in *Happy Days* is very nice, but it doesn't actually show much of me as a performer. It's a vehicle for which I oiled myself up for four years. The experience I had before gave me the ammunition to play this role.

"Being on *Happy Days* has helped me a great deal. I've been lucky to be playing a character who is interested in music. Also, I've been lucky enough to be stronger off the show than on it. I can go on other shows and leave Potsie behind. You're in trouble if the character you play is stronger than you are. At first, everybody thought I was like Potsie in real life. But that's something that happens to everybody when they're playing a role."

Anson started out writing lyrics to songs. "And I was very bad," he confessed. "I wrote gushy, gushy, me, me, me type of stuff. Then I began to write about things that would interest other people, too. Now I have a partner, a fine composer named Janet Glazener. I'm a bad technical musician. I write the words and indicate the melody. She finishes off the music and I finish off the words. We've formed our own recording company. Other companies have offered me big money to record junk. I said no and it was worth the wait — now I can have creative control.

"I've done a few songs I'm proud of," Anson added. "One of them is 'Every Moment of Your Life.' I'd like to come out with a strong single like 'Tie A Yellow Ribbon,' so that my identity becomes that of a songwriter and singer rather than Potsie from *Happy Days*. Right now I'm recognized primarily because of the show. That's great, but I'd like to switch over and be known for my music."

A number of people have helped him in his career, Anson said. One of them was Fred Ebb, a well-known lyricist who wrote *Cabaret*, *Chicago*, and other hit Broadway shows. "He's worked with me and given me confidence," Anson noted. "He taught me to be honest on the stage. He works with *top* people. I've really been lucky. He told me to be a 'people performer.' I want to do things in a way that will make people happy. I can't solve people's problems, but I can help them forget their problems for awhile.

"When I'm in the dumps," Anson admitted, "I feel better after I hear someone I really like. I feel better able to handle my problems. That's what I want to do to others — make them feel terrific. Not with a message necessarily — except maybe peace and love.

"I've really been lucky with my singing career. I've been doing concerts all over the country. I did several Mac Davis shows, I've been a regular on *The Hollywood Squares*, and I've been on the Merv Griffin and Dinah Shore shows a number of times. Now I'm doing major variety shows."

I asked Anson if he ever got nervous doing a TV talk show. He laughed. "I used to get like crazy sick!" he replied. "But now I've found that being on shows like that is really my cup of tea. Now I'm more nervous about doing a terrific job than being on the show. I just say whatever comes to mind. I'm not a comedian. I have no talent for comedy. I can't work with a planned standup comedy routine."

Anson is young, handsome, and single — and he has built up quite a reputation for being a ladies' man. "Is there a special girlfriend?" I asked him.

"All my girlfriends are special!" he answered quickly. "I like to do many things, especially outdoor things like hiking or horseback riding. I'm also a movie freak."

That reminded Anson of one aspect of his business which he doesn't like. "I'm not an awards freak, though," he declared. "Most awards are baloney. The important thing is to do a good job. Awards are superficial. I just don't enjoy them."

"I went to the Emmy Awards once. I spent $50 for a ticket, I put on my tux — and then I ended up sitting in the balcony where we had to watch a TV monitor to see the stage! I thought, 'What am I doing here?' I was with Liza Minnelli and Lorna Luft. They felt the same way I did. It was the most boring piece of junk I've ever tried to sit through. We left and went to McDonald's for dinner. As an artist, you've got to stay away from all that awards junk. If you win, it's fine, but people make more of it than they should. When you become famous, the whole celebrity syndrome starts. You become a product. People make money off you. I don't like that, but you can't fight it."

When I talked to him, Anson was looking forward to going to Hawaii. "It will be my first vacation in two years," he said. "I'm taking my parents to Hawaii for 10 days. We're going to Honolulu, to Maui, and to the big island of Hawaii." Anson laughed. "I waited for three years to get a gig in Hawaii. Now I'm paying for the trip and I've had offers for two jobs!"

Anson's career has had its ups and downs, he admitted. "There have been times when I was discouraged," he said, "but I've always had confidence in myself. Nothing cheers me up faster than performing for people. When I was just beginning, if I got depressed I would go somewhere and sing for free. I never really thought of doing anything else. I would never be happy as a teacher or a civil service employee, so I figured, why not do this? Why not be a performer?"

Anson isn't home a great deal. When he is, he's happy to have a chance to catch up on his sleep. "I live in a really neat house in Glendale," he said. "It's an old house. It's like an English tudor castle. It has five apartment units. I have one of the units and it's great. It's very secluded."

Sometimes his travels have led to amusing incidents. On one visit to New York, he was driving down Broadway and made what could have been a terrible mistake. "I stopped for a pedestrian — like we do in California," he recalled. "You could smell rubber burning and hear brakes being slammed on for a mile back. A woman stuck her head in the window and yelled, 'Are you crazy?'" Anson smiled and shook his head.

"This is a happy time for me," he added thoughtfully. "It is also a very spiritual time — a time for re-evaluating myself and my priorities. It's a heavy time, a time for making major decisions. All of a sudden you find yourself on top and you think, 'Holy cow! What do I do? Who do I turn to?' You begin to ask questions and to answer them — and all of that is part of growing.

"You begin to learn that happiness in life is a very basic thing. It's the basic things that make you happy. I'm glad I've learned that at the age of 26. If I lost everything tomorrow, I'd still be happy because of what I've been able to do these past few years. Fame and money are not important. Too many people are too concerned about such things. They're too materialistic, and that's all baloney. That's not a happy way to live. That's why so many people have ulcers. Their body is giving them a message.

"Basically, I'd like to tell kids what they have, not what they don't have," Anson stressed. "Kids are so much more aware and more human than when I was growing up. They have been through so many crises that many of them have kind of gone back to nature. I've learned a lot from them.

"You can learn from nature. You can't base your life on man-made things. You're going to be happiest with God's things. That's what I've learned. Everyone is someone. Everyone is very important. Everyone has a reason for being here. You need family, friends, God, love, and nature. All the rest are tools."

Anson has worked hard to become a

successful actor and singer. He's not sure he should be getting all the attention he is just for playing Potsie Weber. "I think all of us are getting too much adulation for doing a show like *Happy Days*," he said. "It's not really that hard to do. The real genius is in the writing and the directing. But now that we have all this adulation, we must do something to deserve it. That's why I'm working hard on my music.

"I don't base Potsie on the 1950's. The language, the walk, the attitude might be 1950's. But Potsies, Fonzies, Richies, and Ralphies are all universal characters. There's no set year for them. I think that's why the series has been so successful. Kids can relate to us because that's how they and their friends are today! Potsie is vulnerable. He's the product of a simpler era. Kids today really feel so terrific about themselves. They're more aware of their world. That gives them confidence — and the ability to laugh at some of the things they have in common with Potsie.

"There's a little of me in Potsie," Anson added, "but not much. Me? I'm not a Potsie!"

Donny Most: Just Like Being Back in Erasmus Hall High School

Donny Most was headed out of town. He called, somewhat out of breath, just before taking off. "I'm getting on a plane for Cedar Rapids, Iowa," he said. "I'm going there to do a muscular dystrophy telethon." I could just see him shut in a phone booth at the airport and the plane taking off without him. Fortunately, that didn't happen. Cedar Rapids wanted Donny Most — alias Ralph Malph — to help raise money for a worthy cause. And Donny would be there.

Donny has been having a great time since he got the part in *Happy Days*. "When I first started doing the show my part was pretty small," he told me. "It was almost like they wrote it in at the last minute. I tested for the role of Potsie, but they wanted Anson for that, so they created Ralph for me.

"Now I'm one of the four guys and my part has gotten a lot bigger," Donny said enthusiastically. "I've had a lot more opportunity to develop the character and really let it grow. It's given me a chance to exercise my acting craft. Otherwise the role would be little more than telling a few jokes now and then. People really know who Ralph is now. We've had a few shows where some of Ralph's problems have been explored. I really love doing *Happy Days*!"

Donny has wanted to be an actor ever since he was a child and saw the movie, *The Jolson Story*. When he was 15, he got his first real taste of show business. He sang and danced with a specialty review featuring young people on the Catskills circuit in New York. The group appeared in big hotels throughout the Catskills. He may not have been Al Jolson, but Donny was getting his start — and he was singing and dancing his heart out!

Donny grew up in Brooklyn, New York. After graduation from Erasmus Hall High School, he enrolled at Lehigh University in Bethlehem, Pennsylvania, as a business major.

But show business had gotten to him by

then. While still on the Catskills circuit, he had been seen by a New York agent who was convinced he could broaden his horizons by becoming an actor. Donny was eager to try. He studied in New York with drama coach Elinor Raab and at various workshops around the city.

He decided to drop out of college. In August, 1973, he headed for Los Angeles. He played his first TV roles in episodes of *Room 222* and *Emergency*. And then *Happy Days* came along. Donny eased into the role of the jaunty, wise-cracking high school senior just as if he'd never left Erasmus Hall!

"The show has gotten so much better," Donny exclaimed. "Doing it in front of an audience makes a tremendous difference. It gives the actors and the writers a chance to change and improve.

"Also," Donny added, "some stations are showing reruns of *Happy Days* during the day. That means we're reaching even more people who may then tune in at night.

"Moving Fonzie to the Cunninghams' also increased the potential of the series. Doing that meant Fonzie could be prominent in more of the shows."

Playing Ralph Malph has given Donny's career a tremendous boost. He has already co-starred in his first motion picture, *American Dream*, with Cloris Leachman. He also portrayed Tom Sawyer in ABC's *Huckleberry Finn*, a TV special in which Ron Howard played the title role. And he made his TV singing debut, he said, on *The Merv Griffin Show*. It's no wonder he's out of breath at times — and he wants to keep it that way.

"I'm working on some music now," he explained. "I love to sing. I'm working with arrangers on songs to do. I'd love a nightclub act — but only if it didn't get in the way of acting. I don't want anything to hurt that. I'd like to do another movie or a play. I'm taking singing and speech lessons. The voice is so important, especially if you want to do the classics someday."

But, meanwhile, Donny's plane was ready to leave. He had a telethon to do. But he left on a happy note: "All of us on *Happy Days* get along so well," he said. "It makes it fun to go to work. We are really good friends!"

Fonzie For President?

It was a warm, sunny, spring morning. I gave the taxi driver the address of Henry Winkler's Hollywood apartment. "I've only been driving three days," he announced cheerfully. "Do you know where it is?"

Fortunately, I did. "Yes," I said. "I'll direct you. It's easy." Why not, I thought. It was a beautiful morning. Besides, I wanted to get there. I was due at 10:00 a.m. I didn't want to be late. Henry isn't one who sleeps until midafternoon. I was eager to see him. This was the spring when *Happy Days* — and Fonzie — had soared in popularity. Everything had clicked into place. My friend Henry had become a major star since I'd seen him last.

I arrived 10 minutes early. The apartments in the small complex were set around a modest-sized swimming pool. I sat by the pool for a minute and enjoyed the warm sunshine. I had said I would wait there to meet a network publicist who is a good friend of Henry's. It was a wait I enjoyed. Few people were around. It was a quiet, settled kind of place — a far cry from the swinging singles places scattered elsewhere around the city. Here there was a feeling of relaxation. No razzle-dazzle. No loud parties. No forced gaiety. You could almost imagine The Fonz doing his ironing in this kind of place!

Henry, I knew, wasn't going to live here much longer. He had bought a house in the San Fernando Valley. Not in the posh Beverly Hills or Bel Air areas? No, Henry had become a superstar, but he hadn't let that change his whole life-style.

Henry's apartment was on the ground floor behind the pool. We walked around promptly at 10:00 a.m. Henry threw open the door and greeted us with a big smile. I knew, even then, that success *hadn't* changed this talented young actor. I would have been amazed if it had.

The part of the apartment I could see

consisted of a living room and a small kitchen. It was cluttered with books and plants. The front window looked out toward the pool. A couch was at the left, the kitchen at the right, a beanbag chair in the corner. ("Ron Howard gave me that chair for my birthday last year," Henry said.)

I asked Henry about his new house. Was he doing the decorating? "I picked out the colors for two rooms," he replied. "Both colors were wrong, so the rooms had to be repainted." He smiled. "It's a 40-year-old, medium-sized house. I don't have much furniture that I'll take with me. I do have the beanbag chair and a big four-poster bed. One reason I bought the house is because it has space you can walk to. It has an upstairs. I must go upstairs to go to bed."

Henry paused and looked around. "Would you like some tea?" he asked. Henry makes great herb tea with honey — and he is thoughtful enough to share it with visitors. (That is not true of many other performers I have met. There are those who invite you to their homes at lunchtime and then never offer you anything to eat or drink.)

Henry made the tea, settled down in a chair, and got back to the subject of his house. I knew Henry had grown up in an apartment in New York. Where had he gotten used to living in a house with an upstairs?

"My family has a house at Lake Mahopac, New York," he said. "When I was growing up, we spent summers and weekends there."

Henry has always admitted that growing up — for him — wasn't easy. But he understands his family better today. He had been in New York to visit them not long before.

"I wanted to surprise them," he said. "I went for my sister's 35th birthday. I arrived in town the day before the party. I didn't want my parents to see me, even though I stayed in the same neighborhood. I kept running into people I knew, but I asked them all not to tell. And they didn't! The next day, after the party had been going for about an hour and a half, I walked in and surprised everyone. Were they surprised! I felt terrific!"

I hadn't seen Henry for 10 months. His life, since then, had been topsy-turvy. "Things are wild now," he admitted. "The show's popularity has tripled! I can't tell you why. I guess it's time for *Happy Days* to be popular! The entire family is watching it, from babies to grandparents!"

Henry himself had been in orbit. He had returned four days earlier from a trip to Australia. "I went there to present the awards for their top TV shows. I gave 10 awards." He laughed. He'd enjoyed it. And why not? Henry has great warmth and sensibility — and he's smart enough to enjoy an invitation to visit Australia.

Australia buys some U.S. TV shows, Henry explained, but the awards were only for programs made in Australia. Thus, neither Henry nor *Happy Days* won anything. But if Henry ever does win an award, he'll soon have a place to put it. "My new house has a mantel over the fireplace," he said with a smile.

"Do you have any trophies to put on it?" I asked.

"Yes," Henry said with a grin, pointing to a baseball sitting on a table nearby. "I'm the pitcher for the *Happy Days* softball team. I pitched a no-hit game so they gave me the ball." Then he pointed to an autographed football sitting in the corner behind my head. "The Green Bay Packers sent me that ball," he explained. "I did a promo for their telethon."

Fonzie's extraordinary popularity has led people all over to come up with some wild ideas. What about the biggest prize of all? It was an election year. Would The Fonz run for President? The idea was suggested by a newspaper columnist on the East Coast. The columnist polled his readers. The results? "Ford got 3 votes, Reagan got 2, Fonzie got 430," Henry said.

But Henry wanted to make it perfectly clear. "The Fonz is not running for President," he declared. "But if he were, his slogan would be: 'The Country Needs a Lube Job.'"

The Fonz would get a lot of votes in any election. His fans number in the millions. I asked Henry if they had begun to get out of hand. "Fans don't get out of hand," he responded. "There are always those who want to be hostile, but most of them are terrific. It's the people making money from you who get out of hand," he added. "I'm always being ripped-off. All those things on the market with Fonzie's picture on them are a rip-off. They're junk. The only authentic thing is a T-shirt I designed. I did it because I think people should get quality."

He disappeared for a moment and came back carrying a T-shirt. Fonzie's picture was on the front and the back. Lettering on the back said The Fonz. It was much nicer than anything I'd seen in any stores. "The color of the lettering will change every 1,200 shirts," Henry said. "That way only a limited number of people will have the same color."

Henry cares about his fans — and he doesn't like to see them paying big money for products that aren't any good.

Even in Australia, he was mobbed by fans. "I couldn't walk down the street without being mobbed," he said. "While I was there, I also did a public relations job for the show. I went to the TV station and persuaded them to show *Happy Days* at a different time. They were showing it at 5:30 p.m. I talked them into showing it later in the evening.

"I also taught them my name — Henry Winkler — in seven days. They went from posters of Fonzie to posters of Henry Winkler. During my stay there, I went to the outback where the land is red and green and rolls on forever, and where aborigines have lived for 4,000 years.

Small communities are scattered around. I rode a camel, I herded cattle, I made cowboys' bread. I heard fascinating talks about the history and artifacts of the aborigines."

Henry had only been home for a few days. The excitement of the trip hadn't worn off. "In Melbourne I received more gifts in three days than I've received in 30 years of birthdays — jewelry, books, a stuffed koala bear, a belt, and at least six dozen flowers, all of which arrived one at a time. Some of the presents I brought home. Others I gave to people to remember me by. I saw one real kangaroo in the outback; I brought a stuffed one home.

"For the first time in my life, I traveled by myself. It was an interesting experience. I have distant relatives in Australia. They are a fabulous married couple, with three kids. I ate them out of house, home — and paté. I'd finish off the paté before anybody else got to it!" Henry laughed.

Henry is fun to talk to. His interests are wide-ranging. He is very perceptive — of himself and of those around him. "When you travel alone," he pointed out, "you find that you're made of stronger stuff than you thought. You have to be strong to travel by yourself. But it's a lonely thing to do. It's probably easier for me because I can meet people pretty quickly. But cultures and attitudes are different in other countries. People everywhere are really about the same, but there are always those little differences in culture — and even language — that you have to watch.

"While I was in Australia, I did a radio show with people calling in. I found that works better than my sitting there being interviewed by a disc jockey. One girl called in and used a word that is acceptable in this country. After I repeated it, I found it has a different meaning in Australia!

"There are disadvantages to traveling alone," he stressed. "It's lonely because you are having such a heightened experience. I was alone — even though women camped outside my hotel and sang songs and yelled my name. I had planned on going to Tahiti for a few days, but those plans fell through. I ended up spending two hours there, very early in the morning, and that was all."

"In The Midst of All That Craziness, a Human Being"

After all is said and done, *Happy Days* isn't popular because it's set in the 1950's or because it's nostalgic. Nostalgia — or looking back at a time that has passed — may make you tune in to a show once, but it won't bring you back week after week. *Happy Days* has much more than nostalgia going for it.

The Cunningham family has great appeal. They are the family we would all like to have. There are no ugly scenes. There are no problems that can't be solved. They treat each other with respect — and with humor. In one episode, Joanie wrote secret letters to Potsie, and Richie discovered it. "I'm not going to laugh at you," he told his younger sister. "Yes, you will," she said. But Richie didn't laugh at her. He put his arm around her. "It's part of growing up," he assured her. And then Joanie asked the question that every young person has asked at one time or another: "But why does it have to hurt so much?"

Growing up does hurt. And having brothers and sisters has its bad moments, too. Sometimes it's a pain, in fact. But anyone lucky enough to have brothers and sisters knows there are also the good times, the happy times. Those are the times we share with the Cunningham family.

Fonzie couldn't live with them and not change. He could not remain outside their moments of laughter and tenderness. He adapted in his own way. Most of the changes came not from the scripts, but from Henry's understanding of the character he plays. Henry knows Fonzie better than anyone else. He knew when it was time for Fonzie to change.

"Fonzie had to change," Henry said. "As you know, we do the show in front of a studio audience now. Fonzie couldn't stay as quiet and aloof in front of an audience. Also, being at the Cunninghams' changed things. We had to find a man who was cool but who had more of a sense of humor. I was very nervous about making any changes. Change is always scary, but it's the foundation of growth. You must overcome fear.

"We never really talked about making changes. Things just came up. How do I as an actor solve the problem of Fonzie wearing glasses? How does The Fonz react to a truth serum — such as jumping over 14 garbage cans on his motorcycle, ending up in the hospital, and discovering that that wasn't really cool at all? Fonzie also started to laugh this year, which he had never done before. He might have smiled before, but that was all. I'm always afraid to make changes," Henry added, "but that doesn't stop me from making them. I never know what I'm going to do until I do it. We rehearse Monday through Thursday; then sometimes I find myself making changes when we film the show on Friday."

Happy Days was not in production at the time Henry and I were talking. That's why Henry had had time to visit Australia. He was looking forward, in the weeks ahead, to having time to relax and to move to his new house.

We were talking in the living room of

his apartment, and Henry was suddenly reminded of some "bachelor chores" he was trying to get caught up on. He excused himself and went outside briefly. He returned with clothes he'd just taken out of the dryer. As we talked, he spread socks and shirts around the room to finish drying. We went back to the subject of *Happy Days*.

"At the very base of it all," Henry noted, "I'm an actor. I'm paid to do a job and I will do the best job I possibly can. That's why I went to school for nine years. I love doing it. I'm complete when I do it. I'm happy when I'm working. I'm not here to fill time or space. They hired my imagination. Part of the training of an actor is learning how to release your imagination. I didn't know all this was going to happen.

"For the first time in two years, I'm proud. I used to be defensive about my success. I was afraid I'd get cocky. Now I'm beginning to relax. I created this character out of my imagination. I know what I'm doing."

Henry paused. He is sure of himself, but he is not cocky. "If the humanity goes out of the character of Fonzie, his popularity will drop like a hot potato," he said. "One reason Fonzie is popular is that in the midst of all that craziness there's a human being. If I become a caricature, it's all over. An actor is good when his soul is injected into the character. If I lost that, I'd be giving up the ship; I'd be an imitation of myself.

"Keeping the character true is what's important. Mrs. Cunningham, for example, can get away with some things that the others can't. She's the only one who can call Fonzie, Arthur. That happened by mistake — and I knew it was right. Now she kisses me good-bye. The Cunninghams are the family Fonzie never had. Everybody needs a family."

Henry's own family, I knew, had brought him up in a comfortable, middle-class New York environment. Henry didn't know anyone like Fonzie when he was growing up. "In creating Fonzie, I didn't draw from my own experience," he acknowledged, "except for the humanity that's in everybody. I read about people like Fonzie in the newspaper. They were called the Rocks.

"I also didn't know anything about motorcycles," Henry admitted. "They're very dangerous. For those who do like motorcycles, all I can do is wish them health. Fonzie isn't a bad image, though," he added thoughtfully. "Nobody's dropped out of school because of him. Whenever I talk to kids I tell them to stay in school. Fonzie is loved because he projects the confidence of being right. That is a quality that all people want desperately."

During the time since I had seen him last, Henry had made the ABC movie, *Katherine*. "That's my proudest moment on film," he said. "I also did several telethons and made a couple of personal appearances. But I'd still like very much to do a feature film. I think about it, but I have no scripts at the moment. I just have to be patient and hope they'll come in. You have to keep hoping — you never know what's going to happen in this business."

Henry's face suddenly lit up. "Yesterday my idol called," he exclaimed. "Phoebe Snow! She's one of the great singers of our generation. She called from her home in New Jersey. I had mentioned her, and how much I liked her, on the Dinah Shore show. Would you like to hear her?"

He jumped up and went over to his

stereo to put on a record. Her lovely, deep, melancholy voice filled the room. We sat in silence and listened. Henry obviously knew the record well.

The phone rang several times while we were sitting there. One of the callers was Tom Bosley — "Mr. C." of *Happy Days*. Another time Henry answered the phone and no one was there. "That's why I'm going to have an answering service screen my calls once I get into the new house," he said.

While the music played in the background, I asked Henry what had been the best thing about the past year. "The best thing was that I survived it," he replied. "No, everything was the best," he added. "On the other side of all the aggravation is the fact that I'm a success, the show is a success, and I'm doing what I want to do — working. Also, I was invited to Australia; I lost weight; I saw Phoebe Snow at the Roxy. I lost weight because the camera puts 10 pounds on you."

"Henry," I asked, "have you any regrets?"

I wasn't sure he had heard me. He sat back and looked thoughtful. Was he thinking or listening to the music? He was thinking. "No," he finally said quietly, "I have no regrets."

"Do you have someone to share all this with?" He looked at me for a moment and then got up and started walking around the room. "You never really have anyone to share it with," he responded. "Stardom is not easy to handle. It's such a heightened life-style. Unless someone else is living it themselves, they can never understand what you're going through. Things happen so quickly, so fast. People leading normal lives may have something great happen to them once a month or so. Now, every day something happens to me. You want to tell your friends, but they are standing outside it. You know you can begin to drive them crazy by telling them everything — so you stop sharing things, and that's very difficult.

"At this moment in my life I'm being very indulgent," Henry said. "That's why I've been doing several interviews a day. That's my opportunity to get all of this out of my body. I can say, 'Yes, this is happening,' and that releases the pressure. If I kept it all inside me, you'd have to scrape me off the walls!

"I'd like to give myself some time to sit

quietly. So much has happened to me that I need privacy to keep everything in proportion. I have no special girlfriend at the moment. Music is still very important to me. I get a kick out of meeting rock stars."

Music reminded him that a reporter from a music magazine had taped an interview with his mother in New York and then sent Henry a copy of the tape. "Want to hear some of it?" Henry asked. "It's wonderful."

He put the tape on — and it *was* wonderful. Henry's mother, speaking with a heavy German accent, was proudly telling the reporter how Henry had been brought up, how he had gone regularly to the synogogue as a child, how well-liked he had been, and so on. She told of visiting the *Happy Days* set — and of cousins all around the country, several of them teachers, whose students didn't believe they were really related to The Fonz. His mother hadn't wanted Henry to be an actor, but she was proud now. Henry smiled as he listened to her.

One of the things that is most important to Henry today is maintaining his own identity. He's been on a national campaign, of sorts, to remind people that he isn't Fonzie. He is Henry Winkler.

"Henry Winkler is real," he said vehemently. "Fonzie is my fantasy. I don't want to be like him in real life. No one can be like him in real life. He is only from my imagination. He is a job to play, but playing him is still work. When anyone calls me Fonzie, I stop them and say, 'My name is Henry.' I risk embarrassing them, but it's a risk I take. My life is more important than getting lost in someone else's name. My name is Henry. That's what I was born as and what I grew up as. My name is only an identity for what I have developed into. I have not developed into Fonzie. I have developed into Henry!

"In Australia, my campaign worked. As soon as I got off the plane I saw a headline which read: 'Call Me Henry, Says The Fonz.' " He pulled out the newspaper and showed me. "One of the TV stations here in Los Angeles always refers to me as Henry Fonzie Winkler. They won't give me the distinction of using my right name! I'm making progress in my campaign," Henry added. "Now about 90 percent of my fan mail says 'Dear Henry,' not 'Dear Fonzie.' "

Henry has turned down very lucrative offers for TV commercials because he refuses to play Fonzie any place but on *Happy Days*. He could be making thousands, if not millions, of dollars playing Fonzie in commercials, but he won't do it. He won't exploit the character he has so carefully created.

Henry Winkler Made It Work

My meeting with Henry was drawing to a close. "Can you ever imagine getting tired of playing Fonzie?" I asked him.

He smiled. "Sure, you can get tired of playing one character for five years. I didn't train for nine years to play one character. I have two more years to play him.

"We'll continue to make changes in the show. Richie, Potsie, and Ralph will graduate from high school and go on to a junior college in town. And Fonzie will change. Characters have to change."

As we walked toward the door, Henry pointed down at two big boxes filled with letters. "I've read 100,000 fan letters," he said. "But now I get 11,000 letters every two weeks. I used to read them all, but I can't keep up anymore."

I was reminded of something producer Tom Miller had told me about Henry. "He cares deeply about what he's doing," Miller said. "He is passionate if he believes someone wants him to do something that isn't right. Nobody ever says to him, 'You have to do this,' because he is almost always right. He knows the character he is playing."

And Henry has been successful. Through talent, training, experience, and hard work, he has created a character who makes us laugh and makes us care.

As Henry and I said good-bye, we were both reminded of the first time we had met on that cold winter day in New York. We had been strangers then. We parted now as friends, and I wished him well.